A BOOT UP

# THE NORFOLK BROADS
## BOOK ONE

Tony Rothe

First published in Great Britain in 2011

British Library Cataloguing-in-Publication Data
A CIP record for this title is available from the British Library

ISBN 978 0 85710 017 7

**PiXZ Books**
Halsgrove House, Ryelands Industrial Estate,
Bagley Road, Wellington, Somerset TA21 9PZ
Tel: 01823 653777
Fax: 01823 216796
email: sales@halsgrove.com

An imprint of Halstar Ltd, part of the Halsgrove group of companies
Information on all Halsgrove titles is available at: www.halsgrove.com

Printed and bound in China by Toppan Leefung Printing Ltd

## Contents

The Norfolk Broads

# How to use this book

## The Area

The area known as the Norfolk Broads, or just Broadland, contains some of the most remote scenery you will find anywhere, and yet you are rarely more than 10 miles from the port and major resort of Great Yarmouth, or the historic city of Norwich. Much of the area's charm, stems from its isolation and inaccessibility. Many of the Broads themselves are only accessible by boat, with few footpaths and even fewer roads taking you alongside the Broads themselves. Many of these walks take you along riverbanks, giving you glimpses of open water of the Broads where possible. Covering over 300 sq km, the Norfolk and Suffolk Broads together form Britain's largest area of wetland, including 43 separate Broads and 6 rivers, offering 125 miles of lock-free navigation. The Norfolk and Suffolk Broads Act of 1988 effectively gave the area National Park status, but with its own tailor-made legislation to protect both the diverse wildlife, and navigation interests.

The ten walks in this little book explore the area around four Norfolk rivers, the Yare, the Bure, the Ant and the Thurne, and the title of each walk indicates which river it is based around. The routes taken by these waterways are described as the walks unfold. The landscape includes rivers, shallow lakes, woodland, fens, grazing marshes and farmland, usually in a context of startling beauty, and with an amazing variety of wildlife habitats – walks to appeal to everyone.

## The Route

This book is not aimed at serious long distance walkers. You won't necessarily need long woolly socks, plus-fours, heavy rucksacks, or even proper walking boots, although waterproof footwear is recommended for most of the walks, especially in winter, or in wet weather.

All the walks are circular, ie they bring you back to your starting point, and are between 1.3 and 4 miles long.

When walking casually you will be doing about 2 miles per hour, a more purposeful pace will get you along at about 3 miles an hour, so the shortest walks need take you no more than about half an hour, whereas the longest can take you over two hours. And it's difficult to get lost — Riverbank paths leave little choice but to follow the route of the river, but carrying a compass is always a good idea, as the direction you should be walking is always given.

## The Maps

Sketch maps are included, but if you want a definitive map, then the Ordnance Survey Explorer maps (1:25000 series) are unbeatable and are recommended. All the walks in this book are to be found on map OL40 The Broads. Starting points are given, together with the British Grid reference which will enable you to find the spot on any Ordnance Survey map, and the nearest postcode, so that you can even use your SatNav! Each starting point provides somewhere to park, but in a few cases there may be a parking fee. Public Transport is rather sparse in this part of the world, but where buses pass near the start of a walk, this information is given.

Nearest toilets and refreshments are suggested, but you must realise that many places are seasonal, so please don't complain if the ice cream man isn't where you expect to find him on a bitterly cold Tuesday morning in February!

The difficulty of each walk is indicated by a "boot" rating, based mainly on the quality of the paths, the gradients, and even the likely amount of mud! However, these are based on Norfolk standards: compared to many walks in the Lake District or Pennines, the walks in this book would probably all rank as "1 boot". Most of these walks are not suitable for push-chairs, but this information is also given for each walk.

So, please use this little book to explore a very beautiful corner of a wonderful and varied part of the UK, and have fun doing so.

## Key to Symbols Used    Walk Locations

### Level of difficulty:

Easy 🍂

Fair 🍂 🍂

More challenging 🍂 🍂 🍂

### Map symbols:

🚗  Park & start

—— Road

----- Footpath

■  Building / Town

+  Church

🍺  Pub

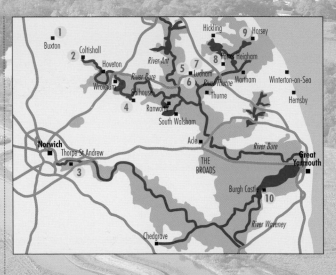

# 1 Bure – Buxton: Riverbank to Oxnead

*Riverbanks, fields and a little railway*

This is a pleasant walk in the north-west corner of Broadland, which starts by a narrow gauge railway, then proceeds through the village of Buxton, and alongside a beautiful stretch of the River Bure, returning across the fields to the car park. The River Bure rises in North Norfolk - then heads broadly south-east, becoming navigable at Coltishall. It flows through Wroxham and Horning before meandering across the northern edge of the Halvergate Marshes and joining the River Yare at the tip of Breydon Water, near Yarmouth. The village of Buxton dates from Roman times, and was referred to in the Domesday book as Buckestuna, meaning the town of Buck. The village is commonly referred to as Buxton Lamas, although Lamas is actually the adjoining village to the east of the river.

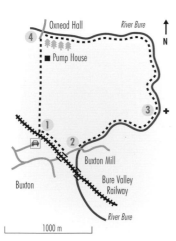

Oxnead Hall
River Bure

Pump House

Buxton Mill

Bure Valley Railway

Buxton

River Bure

1000 m

**Level:** ♥ ♥
**Length:** 2.8 miles
**Terrain:** Road through village, grassy paths along riverbank, good paths through fields.
**Start/park:** Bure Valley Walk car park in village. (free)
**Map ref:** TG 232229 nearest postcode NR10 5ET
**Refreshments:** Black Lion Pub in village.
**Toilets:** None.
**Transport:** Bure Valley Railway to Aylsham or Wroxham.
**Pushchairs:** With difficulty.

(1) From the car park, go through the gate and cross the narrow gauge railway line. You will be adjacent to the Bure Valley Railway's Buxton halt. Turn right to go south-east along the path beside the track. When you get to the bridge over the road, go down the steps to the left onto the road, then turn left to head north-east along the pavement towards the mill, where the road goes over the river.

(2) Turn left just before "Gullane House" to head east along a path marked "Riverside Walk". The mill continued in use until 1953, then continued trading as a mill and then a gallery and restaurant until destroyed by fire in 1991. After restoration to its original

*A steam train from the Bure Valley Railway crosses the River Bure close to Buxton (courtesy Mike Page).*

*The mill on this spot was recorded in the Domesday Book of 1085, but the current building dates from 1772. It was a clever design as it was worked partly by the river Bure passing under its wheels and partly by a canal brought from Oxnead which turned an overshot wheel.*

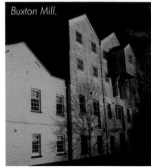

Buxton Mill.

*The River Bure at Lammas.*

18th century design it became a hotel and is now private flats. Soon you will reach the River Bure, and you will need to follow the riverbank path for about 2 miles, over several stiles and through open meadows.

(3) You will soon be alongside Lammas Church across the river, and also Lammas Hall. You will cross the path of a Roman road, but

*Tree-lined meadows.*

*Lammas Church.*

*Mute swan.*

this will not be readily apparent. Eventually you will be walking under trees, and then you will reach a small bridge, close to Oxnead Hall. You will have travelled about 2.3 miles.

(4) Turn left along the track here to head south past the pump house on your left. Go through a gap beside the gate, and continue south across the field, crossing a line of vegetation, which probably marks where the Roman Road ran. Continue south alongside a hedge, then another

*Bridge near Oxnead Hall.*

*The Bure Valley Railway is one of the "Big Three" 15-inch lines in Britain, and follows the trackbed of a railway branch line from Aylsham to Wroxham which was opened by the East Norfolk Railway in 1879.*

open field, until you cross the railway line again and return to the car park. The railway became part of the Great Eastern Railway in 1882, and the London and North Eastern Railway in 1923. The line closed to passengers in 1952, but freight traffic continued until 1982. The narrow gauge line was laid in 1989.

*The Bure Valley Railway at Buxton.*

# 2 Bure – Coltishall: Horstead Mill to Little Hautbois

*Riverbank stroll, and a path through fields*

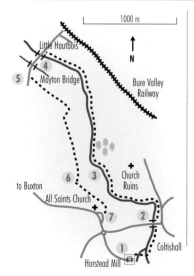

This walk actually starts in the village of Horstead, which adjoins the larger village of Coltishall over the river. The nearby Battle of Britain airfield continued as a major RAF base until 2006. The walk takes you along the riverbank, through the village, and right up to Little Hautbois, returning across fields to Horstead church and then back to the ruins of the watermill. Horstead Watermill was the last mill on the river Bure and to this day marks the end of navigation for the river. There was a mill recorded here in the Domesday Book, but the

**Level:** ♥ ♥ ♥
**Length:** 4 miles
**Terrain:** Grassy and woodland paths.
**Start/park:** Small parking area at the site of Horstead Mill, on Mill Road. (free)
**Map ref:** TG 267194 nearest postcode NR12 7AT
**Refreshments:** Coltishall village – pubs and shops.
**Toilets:** None.
**Transport:** Bure Valley Railway to Wroxham or Aylsham.
**Pushchairs:** No.

most recent structure was built in 1789. The mill, one of the biggest in Norfolk, was gutted by fire during the savagely cold winter of 1963.

From the small car park, head east across the sluice to take the east riverbank towards the village. These ruins are all that is left of the once grand Horstead Mill, and the area is now used for recreation. You will pass some trees growing in a line close

Horstead Mill.

Village sign.

Trees line the riverbank path.

together and soon reach the Norwich road, which you cross.

Then go immediately through the gate straight ahead to follow the path along the north bank of the River Bure. If you are walking in winter, your path will be flanked by snowdrops, and after a while you will

go over a small bridge. You will go past Hautbois (pronounced "Hobbiss") House on a hill to your right. The path then starts to wind somewhat. There will be a dyke to your right, and after a while there will be trees either side of your path. When you reach a marshy area to your right, this was the site of a castle, but there is no sign of it now.

*Looking north-west over Coltishall and the River Bure (courtesy Mike Page).*

*You will see the round tower of the Saxon St Theobald's church, which was apparently deliberately ruined in Victorian times when a new church was built closer to the village centre.*

*Mayton bridge.*

*St Theobald's Church.*

**3** Keeping to the riverbank path, you will go past Church Farm on your right. As the tree cover thins, you will go past a Christmas tree plantation also on your right. You will cross over a small footbridge, and through a chain stile, and will now be out of the trees on to open riverbank. You will see a brick bridge in the distance, and should head for this, roughly north-west. You will cross another footbridge, and shortly another chain stile, and you will emerge onto a lane by a road bridge, and there is evidence that there used to be a ford here. There is also a small parking area – you have travelled 2.1 miles. Mayton Hall will be visible ahead.

**4** Turn left to cross the bridge, and after a few yards along the lane cross another bridge. This second bridge is the ancient Mayton bridge, with its four arches and what appear to be the old toll booths still in place.

**5** You will then turn left at the footpath sign to leave the lane and head south-east along the edge of a field. Continue round the left edge of the next field with marshes still to your

*Wooden footbridge.*

left, and you will see a water tower ahead. Go over a stile and keep to the left edge of the boggy meadow, with a farm to your right. Go over a footbridge, then turn right, following the waymark to continue around the field's left edge, now heading west. Then go left and negotiate a boggy area to cross another stile, then continue south towards a farmhouse and yet another stile, followed by another chain stile. Continue towards the cottages and two more stiles then along a short narrow path to emerge onto a track.

*Path across the fields to Horstead.*

**6** Turn left to head south-east along the track. You have covered 3.3 miles. Very soon take the path which forks to the left, to head east, then cross a meadow to a footbridge in the trees. Head for the church ahead, still going east, and follow a clear path into the churchyard. All Saints, Horstead was built largely in 1879, although the tower is 14th Century. Follow the path through the churchyard, then through the gate to turn right into a layby.

**7** Continue south-east to the road, then on to a junction with the B1150 Norwich Road. Go straight over, and follow the lane opposite, Mill Road, back to where you parked, taking the path left at the waymark and over a bridge into the car park.

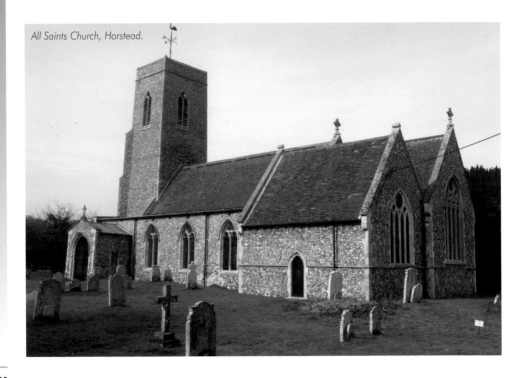

All Saints Church, Horstead.

# 3 Yare – Thorpe St Andrew: Whitlingham Broad and River Yare

*Riverbank and Marsh*

This is the closest walk to the city of Norwich, and its starting point seems somewhat urban. You will however soon be in the countryside, but some buildings will always be in view. The summer route is shorter and prettier than the winter route, but the marsh section will often be flooded in the winter, so the dry route becomes necessary! You will be walking alongside the River Yare, which rises near Dereham, passes south of the city of Norwich, then, about a mile to the west of this walk, picks up the larger Wensum, which is the main river through Norwich. The enlarged Yare then flows broadly east to Great Yarmouth (originally Yare-mouth), where it meets up with the Waveney and the Bure, then flows out to sea.

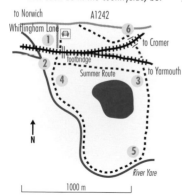

**Level:**

**Length:** 1.6 miles (or less for summer route)

**Terrain:** Riverside paths and tracks.

**Start/park:** There is a short stretch of Whitlingham Lane to the right off the A1042 Yarmouth Road heading out of Norwich. This leads to a level crossing. Find a parking space on that lane without causing an obstruction.

**Map ref:** TG 267084 nearest postcode NR7 0QA

**Refreshments:** Rushcutters pub, and others, in Thorpe St Andrew.

**Toilets:** None.

**Transport:** Many buses along Yarmouth Rd. Rail station (2 miles west)

**Pushchairs:** No.

*You will be close to Whitlingham Country Park, a newly formed open space and broad with woodland, a water-park and a beach, on the site of old quarry workings.*

**①** Head south along the lane towards the level crossing, and you will soon reach a footbridge over the railway, which you should go over, admiring the views from the top. From here the tracks head west into Norwich station, which is the terminus about 2 miles away. Heading east, the track very soon splits, with one route heading north to the coast at Cromer and Sheringham, and the other continuing east to Great Yarmouth or Lowestoft.

*Footbridge over the railway.*

**②** SUMMER ROUTE - Once over the bridge, turn left

before you reach the "no entry" gate to head east along the Station Marshes walk. Then IF THE PATH IS NOT FLOODED, go through the gate onto the marsh following the path between the dykes, and the occasional waymark. The path will bend right, then left over a stile to emerge onto a track where you turn right.

*A spectacular view over Thorpe St Andrew (courtesy Mike Page).*

Muddy path.

River Yare, Towards Norwich

**3** Then follow the lane called Bungalow Lane south until you reach an opening on your right, which leads to a muddy track beside a dyke. Follow this path, which soon bends left, then right to join the bank of the River Yare. Continue along the river-bank as it heads west, then eventually curves round to head north. The country park will be just across the river, but a brand new broad has just been created from quarry workings north of the river to the right of this path, and you will get good views of this as you progress. Your path will lead on to a shingle track which takes you back to the footbridge, which

you cross again to get back to your car. WINTER ROUTE – Once over the bridge, continue south along a shingle track – for the next mile or so you will be walking the end on the "Summer route" in reverse.

Whitlingham Broad.

**4** When you reach the river Yare, follow the path along the river bank as it heads south then curves left to head east, and eventually you will cross a wooden bridge and follow a muddy path to the left of the

Duckboard.

trees alongside a dyke, until you go through an opening onto a lane.

**5** Turn left and head north along the lane until you

reach the railway line. You will have travelled about 0.75 miles. Cross the level crossing with care, then continue north along the lane until you go under a railway bridge.

*Trees growing in the marsh.*

*Norwich-Bound train.*

**6** Then immediately turn left to head west along the lane to the right of the electricity substation, then fork left to drop down to a path between the trees. Continue west along the path as it bends right into Common Lane to reach the main Yarmouth Road. Turn left and follow the road for a short way until you turn left into Whitlingham Lane and back to your car.

# 4 **Bure – Salhouse: To and From Salhouse Broad**

*Paths around the Broad*

The village of Salhouse was recorded in the Domesday Book as being part of the Manor of nearby Wroxham, and the 14th century church, which

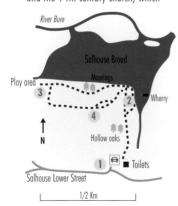

stands to the north of the village is the oldest existing building. Like most of the other broads, Salhouse Broad resulted from medieval peat diggings in the 12th to 14th centuries. The peat, formed from vegetation compressed in the marshy ground, was excavated for fuel, but the proximity of these workings to the river meant they soon flooded, giving us our shallow (about 3m average) but distinctive Broads. This short walk takes you down to the Broad for a pleasant stroll across the grassland alongside the water, then through a

**Level:** 🥾
**Length:** 1.3 miles
**Terrain:** Good track and grassy paths, boardwalk.
**Start/park:** Broads Authority Car Park to the east of Salhouse Lower Street (free)
**Map ref:** TG 320150 nearest postcode NR13 6HG
**Refreshments:** The Bell Pub in village, or Salhouse Lodge about a mile to the west.
**Toilets:** Public toilets in car park.
**Transport:** Anglian coaches 12B. Salhouse railway station 2 miles west.
**Pushchairs:** Yes, but some tricky bits.

small wood and some higher ground overlooking the water, before returning along the path to the car park.

The view east over Wroxham and Hoveton Broads.  Salhouse Broad lies on the far right of the picture where the walk begins (courtesy Mike Page).

*Hollow oak.*

*The path to Salhouse Broad.*

**1** From the car park, take the path past the toilets to soon head north, past some grand hollow oaks, which are a great favourite with children playing hide and seek! After a while, (about 0.3 miles) turn right from your path onto a boardwalk which takes you to the eastern edge of Salhouse Broad. You will be able to make out the remains of a wooden boat in the water, with a tree growing through it. This was a Norfolk sailing wherry, obviously abandoned many years ago and is now well beyond repair. The broad and adjacent river were frequented by many of these distinctive craft from the 19th century, originally for freight, but increasingly

*Eastern end of the Broad.*

*Remains of a wherry.*

serving the early 20th century holiday trade as goods moved onto the faster railway. The smaller motor cruisers started to meet this need more economically from the 1920s, and their modern derivatives are now a common sight on the Broad.

*Motor cruiser on the Broad.*

2 Continue along the boardwalk to the open broad, turning left at the end to head west along the edge of the water, go past the seat, and then to the left of a group of trees. Continue your direction, soon joining a boardwalk, but fork left just before the last mooring, and the path will take you into a children's play area, containing a willow "fedge" which, as the name suggests, is a cross between a hedge and fence, and demonstrates the skill of the willow craftsmen.

3 Return to the boardwalk you came in along, and almost immediately take the path to your right, up into the woods. Continue to the top of the hill, where the path bends to the left to head east, and

Boardwalk north to the Broad.

Willow "Fedge".

there will be views over the fields to your right. Continue east across open grass, past some seats, and you will soon have views over the broad to your left.

(4) At the fork you can take either path, as you will soon descend some shallow steps back to the edge of the broad. You have covered 0.9 miles. Here you turn right to follow the path south, and you will soon be re-tracing your steps back to the car park.

*View north over Salhouse Broad.*

# 5 Ant – Ludham: Ludham Bridge and the River Ant

*Riverbank walk and a stroll through farmland*

This is a lovely walk along the east bank of the river Ant, returning along some farmland paths, and

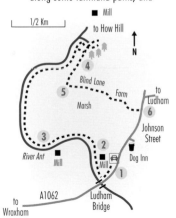

a short stretch of road to finish. The River Ant is the narrowest and northern-most of the Broads' rivers, rising at Dilham, where it connects with the now disused and overgrown North Walsham & Dilham Canal. The Ant's twisting, shallow route takes it through trees and reeds to meet the River Bure about half a mile south of Ludham Bridge. It runs through Barton Broad (to the north of this walk) which is the second largest of the Norfolk Broads, and is home to numerous wildlife, including many species of birds, fish and even otters,

**Level:** 🐾 🐾
**Length:** 3.2 miles
**Terrain:** Grassy paths — uneven and rough in places.
**Start/park:** Small layby on the A1062 to the east of Ludham Bridge. (free)
**Map ref:** TG 373171 nearest postcode NR29 5NX
**Refreshments:** Shop & Restaurant by bridge. Dog Inn at Johnson Street.
**Toilets:** Near layby.
**Transport:** Sanders bus 701 (school term times only)
**Pushchairs:** No.

following a multi-million pound clearwater project a few years ago to remove silt from the broad.

From the layby, head towards the bridge, but before going over it, turn right to follow the east bank of the river, past some moorings. You will soon pass the derelict Ludham Bridge North Drainage Mill, which was a small 3-storey red brick mill, typical of many wind pumps erected from the 18th century to lift the water from the marshes into a lattice of marsh dykes in order to drain the wetlands of the broads area so that they could be used for grazing. By the early 19th century, there were over a hundred of these, soon to be supplemented or replaced by steam pumps, and in the 20th century by diesel powered internal combustion engines, and then by electric pumps. There was also the South mill across the road from the North mill, but this was demolished in the 1960s.

*Ludham Bridge North Drainage Mill.*

*Ludham Bridge (courtesy Mike Page).*

**2** Go through the gate and along the raised bank between the channels of the flood alleviation scheme, with the main river to your left. Although it should be possible to cross to the actual river bank in dry weather, the paths can flood when it is wet. Keep to your path as it follows the river bank,

go through a gate, and eventually you will go past Neave's Mill.

**3** Continue along the path as it bends to head north and eventually east. You have covered about a mile. Turf Fen Drainage Mill will come into view further ahead, with the

*Flood defence bank.*

Norfolk Broads Study Centre at How Hill in the distance. You will reach a waymarked crossing of paths at a small group of trees. Turning left here would take you up to the mill and then to How Hill.

*Neave's Mill*

32

*How Hill and Turf Fen Mill.*

*Above: Moorings at Ludham Bridge.*

*Wildlife on the River Ant.*

(4) Instead, turn sharp right to leave the bank and head south-west with the trees on your left. (It you were able to find it, you could have cut off the corner in dry weather by taking the boggy path to your right before reaching the trees, then right again). You will now be proceeding along Blind Lane, with the path flanked by Norfolk Reed — used for high quality thatching.

5 After a while, when you reach the gate, follow the path to the left along the edge of a field, past some trees on your right, then through a kissing gate, still heading east. You will have fine views over the marsh to your right. Continue along the path, soon between two hedges, and at the junction, continue your easterly direction. You will pass a barn on your left, then through another kissing gate and past some derelict buildings. You will go past Limes Farm and onto a surfaced lane, ignoring the public footpath sign to your left, (unless you wish to extend the walk a little). Continue along the lane, past a dairy farm, possibly seeing some chickens, and assorted farm buildings, until you reach the main road.

*Derelict farm buildings.*

6 You are now back onto the A1062 from Ludham to Wroxham, and you should turn right here, proceeding south with caution as it is a busy road. When you reach Johnson Street you will have a pavement to walk along, which will take you roughly south-west back to the layby where you parked.

## 6 Bure – Ludham: St Benets Abbey and the River Ant

*Riverbank walk and a stroll along a farm track*

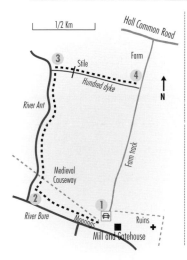

**Level:** 🐾
**Length:** 2.2 miles
**Terrain:** Grassy paths and surfaced farm track.
**Start/park:** Small parking area by the Abbey Gate. Drive to end of track. (free)
**Map ref:** TG 381158 nearest postcode NR12 8NJ
**Refreshments:** Ludham village (1.5 miles to north).
**Toilets:** None.
**Transport:** None.
**Pushchairs:** No.

This pleasant walk starts and finishes at the historic St Benet's Abbey on the banks of the River Bure, and takes you along the east bank of the last bit of the River Ant, alongside Hundred Dyke, and returns along a farm road. St Benet's Abbey sits on a patch of marsh known as Cow Holm, which is technically an island, surrounded by the river and dykes. The monastery was founded in 1020, and was the only one in Britain which survived the Dissolution, because the king exchanged it for lands owned by the Diocese of Norwich instead of closing

it. The abbey itself has now been demolished, but the iconic medieval gatehouse and adjoining eighteenth-century windmill remain.

From the small car park, head south towards the river, then follow a raised path heading west along the new floodbank. Resist the temptation to follow the path past the new moorings on the riverbank, as this is a dead end!

 When the path bends right to head north, you will soon be

*From your path, which lies to the north of the actual river bank, you can just make out the course of an ancient medieval causeway from Horning, which was the original approach road to the abbey when it was built, but it was probably only passable in the summer!*

closer to the river, but this time it is the River Ant, a tributary of the Bure which heads north, to Barton Broad and eventually to Dilham. Stay on your raised path, with water either side of you.

*Sailing dinghy on the Bure.*

*River Ant and marshes.*

*Traditional sailing boat on the River Bure.*

Marshes and reeds.

**4** Turn right onto this track, and head south for about half a mile back to your car.

*The Bishop of Norwich, who can still claim to be Abbot of St Benets, holds an open-air service in this remote spot every summer, with most of the 150-odd attendees arriving by boat.*

**3** After a while the river bends to the left, but you should turn right across a boggy path to a stile, and then onto a grassy path beside Hundred Dyke. You have now travelled about a mile. Continue along this path heading east until you reach the concrete track you drove down to reach the car park.

Hundred Dyke.

*St Benet's Abbey (courtesy Mike Page).*

It is well worth exploring the abbey ruins upon your return. Climb the steps into the Abbey grounds, then follow the path past the remains of the mill (which you are free to enter), and head east for a few hundred yards towards the clearly visible cross. The massive oak cross was brought from the Queen's estate in Sandringham and erected in 1983 on the site of the medieval high altar. The word "peace" is inscribed on the cross, which is appropriate for a place of such isolation and tranquility.

Inside the Mill.

*St Benet's Abbey Gatehouse and Mill – A Broadland icon.*

# 7 Thurne – Ludham: Womack Water and Horse Fen

*Riverbanks and a country track*

**Level:** 💛 💛
**Length:** 2.6 miles (shorter) 3.3 miles (longer)
**Terrain:** Grassy paths and tracks.
**Start/park:** Womack Staithe, along Horsefen Rd, southeast of Ludham village.
**Map ref:** TG 392180 nearest postcode NR29 5QG
**Refreshments:** Ludham village. Shop on staithe. Kings Arms pub.
**Toilets:** Public toilets on staithe.
**Transport:** Sanders bus 701 (school term times only)
**Pushchairs:** with difficulty.

This walk takes you along a country track and down a lane to the

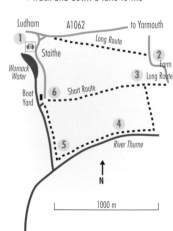

riverside, which you follow right round to a famous boatyard, and then down a lane back to the staithe. Ludham is a medium sized broadland riverside village, straddling the A1062 Wroxham to Yarmouth road. The village includes a 14th century church, pub, village shop, and some tea-rooms. Womack staithe is a few hundred yards from the middle of the village, giving access to Womack Water, and thence the River Thurne. The attractive River Thurne is only 5.7 miles long, running from the tiny Martham Broad only a couple of miles

from the sea, passing through Potter Heigham, and flowing into the Bure just south of Thurne village.

*Looking towards Ludham along Womack Water and the start of the walk (courtesy Mike Page).*

**1** SHORTER WALK: Return to Horsefen Road, and head south-east along the road away from the village. At the end of the road, follow the "Restricted Byway" sign to continue south briefly, then follow the muddy track round to the left to head east. Follow the grassy track, avoiding the mud, and passing some trees on your left, until you eventually emerge onto a surfaced track.

*Boats moored on the River Thurne.*

*Horse Fen.*

**2** Turn right here, through the gateway. **(This is where you meet the longer walk)**

**3** Continue south-east along the straight track - the area to your right is known as Horse Fen. When you reach the electric transformer, turn right over a metal bridge, past Horse Fen pumping station, and up onto the bank of the River Thurne, which will be on your left as you head west.

**4** After a while you will see Thurne Dyke Drainage Mill on your left, and maybe St Benet's Abbey in the distance straight ahead, and

*Womack Water Mill.*

you will soon pass the ruins of the derelict Womack Water Drainage Mill on your right.

**5** Eventually you reach the point where Womack Water meets the Thurne, and your path bends to the right to continue along the bank, this time heading north-west. This path will take you past Hunters Boat Yard back onto Horsefen Road, then you turn left to head north back to the staithe.

**6** Hunters Yard is where Percy Hunter's unique fleet of traditional wooden 1930s sailing yachts is stored and maintained. They are "gaff sloops" with self-tacking jibs and a fixed keel, but no engines! These boats have appeared in the BBC's production of Swallows & Amazons Forever and also Griff Rhys Jones' programme The Rivers and are available for public hire.

*Womack Water.*

*The quay heading (wooden edge) of the staithe was last replaced in 2006, but the work was delayed when the pile driver hit some underground obstructions, which excavations revealed to be oak beams and planks from the remains of a Norfolk Wherry which had evidently been buried on the bank, possibly when the moorings were previously repaired in 1959.*

① **LONGER WALK :-** From the staithe, return to Horsefen Road, and turn left to head north towards Ludham village. Fork right at the "No Entry" sign to reach the main road, then immediately turn right into a bridleway branching off to the right

*Hunters Boat Yard.*

*Womack Staithe.*

*Tree-lined path.*

from the road, heading east. After half a mile follow the waymark to the right of the hedge, as the grassy path continues east.

2   Follow this path to the end, then turn right into the country lane at the end. Proceed south along this lane, curving left past the farm, then right, and continue until the lane ends, then turn right to follow a footpath west, signposted Ludham & Potter Heigham Marsh.

3   The track will soon bend to the left, and you follow this to head south-east. This is where the shorter walk joins from the right, and you should continue from point 3 of those directions.

# 8 **Thurne – Potter Heigham: River Thurne and Horse fen bank**

*A pleasant walk along country paths & roads*

This pleasant walk starts at the historic Potter Heigham Bridge, follows the banks of the River Thurne

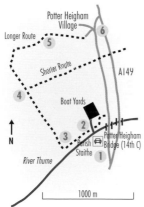

south-west for a while, then paths across marshes and fields before returning via the edge of Potter Heigham village. Potter Heigham is the gateway to the Upper Thurne and the home of the Herbert Woods boatyard founded in 1928. The village itself is ½ mile north-west of the bridge, but it is the river and area around the medieval bridge that attracts visitors. Built, it is believed, in 1385, The bridge is famous not only for its age, but, with a headroom of less than 7ft at high water, notorious for the skill needed to get cruisers and day boats under it!

**Level:** 🥾

**Length:** 1.5 miles (shorter) 2.5 miles (longer)

**Terrain:** Riverside path, country tracks, and roads.

**Start/park:** Parish Staithe, just south of Potter Heigham Bridge, half a mile south-east of Potter Heigham village. Only space for ten cars. The large car park north of the bridge is only for customers of Lathams discount store.

**Map ref:** TG 421184  nearest postcode NR29 5JQ

**Refreshments:** Lathams store near bridge, Broadshaven tavern, Bridge Stores, Fish bar.

**Toilets:** Public toilets near bridge.

**Transport:** Sanders 736 to North Walsham. Mornings only (school bus)

**Pushchairs:** with difficulty.

*Potter Heigham Bridge from the west.*

**1** SHORTER WALK: Cross over to the north of the bridge, then follow the public footpath signs left onto the staithe. Follow the path past the front of the "Broads Tours" building, and take the shingle path alongside the river, heading south-west.

**2** Admire the views as you cross over the footbridge, then continue south along a concrete path

*Herbert Woods' Building*

behind some holiday houses which, unfortunately, restrict your view of the river. This path can flood at high tide, so waterproof footwear is recommended!

**3** Eventually, at a public footpath waymark, take the path to the right through some bushes onto

Horsefen Bank. Follow this good path under a line of trees, heading northwest, for a while until you see a tiny gate on your right. You have covered 1.1 miles. For the longer walk you ignore the gate, and continue northwest, but for the shorter walk turn right here.

*The boatyard at Potter Heigham, near the start of the walk (courtesy Mike Page).*

*Footbridge near start of walk.*

4 You will be on a straight path across the marsh heading north-east, and you will stay on this path for around half a mile until you pass a boatyard and reach the road. This was the main A149 to Yarmouth (including that ancient bridge!) until the new road bridge and bypass were built some years ago. Turn right onto the road, and head back along the road and over the bridge to where you parked.

LONGER WALK: Follow the "shorter walk" directions up to point 4.

4 Continue north-west along Horsefen Bank for a while, still under the trees, then go over a wooden bridge into a field. Then turn right to follow the right edge of the

field. At the next field, turn right again to keep to the way-marked path, now heading North-east, which soon bends to the left.

5 After a while turn right onto a waymarked boardwalk, and proceed east along this path through

*Horsefen Bank.*

*Boardwalk.*

some bushes. Continue as the path goes over a bridge, and soon between some houses and onto a road. A disused mill will just be visible to your right. Turn left here, then right onto Ludham Road. You have now gone 2 miles.

*Marshes near Potter Heigham.*

6   Follow this road, heading south-east, then over the bridge and back to your car.

*There are several ghost stories connected with the bridge. One tells of a coach and horses which thunders down to the bridge on 31st May each year, then plunges off the bridge into the water.*

*Fourteenth-century Potter Heigham Bridge – so low that boats passing through need a pilot.*

# 9 Thurne – Horsey: Horsey Mere and Marshes

*Marsh paths and a stroll following country tracks*

The tiny hamlet of Horsey has been in existence for at least 1000 years, and was recorded in the Domesday Book as having a value of £6:1¼d. The manor

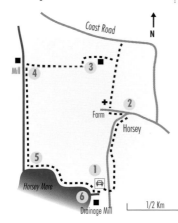

passed through a succession of owners but was frequently flooded and was considered of little value, being known as Devil's Country because of its wildness. The sea bank was repaired, the marshes drained, hedges planted and a road laid in the 19th century, but the area was once again flooded by the sea in 1938. This walk takes you along delightful paths across the marshes and along a path beside Waxham "New" Cut, an 18th century drainage channel, past another drainage mill, and back to the car park past Horsey Mere and Horsey Mill. The Thurne is the nearest river,

**Level:** ♥ ♥
**Length:** 3.0 miles
**Terrain:** River-side paths and tracks.
**Start/park:** Horsey Drainage Mill car park by coast road at Horsey. (National Trust)
**Map ref:** TG 456223 nearest postcode NR29 4EE
**Refreshments:** Kiosk at Horsey Mill (when open). Nelson Head Pub in village.
**Toilets:** Public toilets in car park.
**Transport:** none
**Pushchairs:** with difficulty.

but that only comes up as far as Martham Broad, about 2 miles away – various dykes and drains connect the Broad with Horsey Mere, which is where you will walk.

① Return to the main road, and cross over to go through a wooden gate opposite the NT shop into a field. Turn left to follow a path heading north along the left edge of the field, parallel to the road. After a short while, follow the footpath sign to continue your direction along the roadside verge, with bulrushes on your right.

*Rushes near the road.*

*Horsey Mill at the start of the walk (courtesy Mike Page).*

*Horsey Church.*

**3** Follow the path as it bends left then right past the cottages at Horsey Corner, then go right then left to follow the public footpath sign as it continues west, with the coast road visible to the right. Cross a footbridge, then turn left, with a dyke to your left, then right to continue your westerly direction, with a derelict mill visible ahead.

**2** Go past a 5-bar gate, then left at the post box to follow the sign to the church along Binsley Close. Go past a children's playground on the right, then turn right at the church and go to the end of the lane, continuing north along the public footpath. Continue north to follow the path around the right edge of the field, then left to follow the line of trees west towards some houses.

*A distant view of Brogrove Mill.*

4 Eventually you will go past a waymark, and up onto the bank of the drainage channel known as Waxham New Cut. You will now have a good view of the ruins of Brogrove Drainage mill, built in 1777 to drain the marshes into the New Cut. A modern replacement for the mill is visible to the right of the ruins. Turn left to head south along the bank of the channel, with reeds beside your path.

*Brogrove Drainage Mill.*

*Waxham New Cut, leading to Horsey Mere.*

Boathouse by the Mere.

Horsey Staithe.

(5) Eventually the path bends to the left to leave the main channel. Follow the path along a short boardwalk, then through a gate, then right to head east alongside a fence. Go over a bridge, then turn right to continue alongside the fence, then very soon left to take the path across the meadow to the gate opposite. Go through both gates, along another short boardwalk, up some steps then left to head east, with views of Horsey Mill ahead, and Horsey Mere to your right. You will

pass a thatched boathouse, and emerge onto a drainage channel, heading once more for Horsey Mere and the mill.

(6) Turn left to follow the channel along the staithe, where boats will be moored during the

summer. From the staithe there will be a path back to the car park, but do stop to look round the restored mill before you leave. The mill was restored in 1961 and is now in the ownership of the National Trust, open to visitors in the summer season.

*Horsey Mill is a tower drainage mill, built in the 19th Century on the site of the 200-year old Horsey Black Mill. Rebuilt in 1897 and in 1912 it was once at the cutting edge of drainage mill technology. The Mill ceased working in 1943, when struck by lightning, and the sails were subsequently demolished for safety reasons.*

*Sailing dinghy tied up by Horsey Mill.*

# 10 Yare – Burgh Castle: Roman Castle and Angles Way

*Explore ancient castle ruins and marshes*

This is the most easterly walk in this collection, being only a couple of miles from the sea at Great Yarmouth.

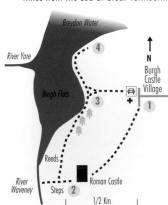

You will take the direct path from the church to the impressive remains of a Roman Castle castle, returning by the marsh path and then, if you wish, taking the riverside path north to enjoy the fabulous views over Burgh Flats, Halvergate Marshes and Breydon Water. In Roman times, the whole of this expansive marsh was a broad estuary leading to the sea, of which Breydon Water is now the only remnant, hence the strategic importance of a castle at this location. The site of what is now the popular resort of Great Yarmouth was then open sea,

**Level:** ♥ ♥
**Length:** 1.0 mile or more
**Terrain:** Fields and riverside paths.
**Start/park:** Church Farm car park, or outside church, at the end of Burgh Castle High Rd.
**Map ref:** TG 476050 nearest postcode NR31 9QG
**Refreshments:** Church Farm (if open) or pub in village
**Toilets:** None.
**Transport:** First Eastern Counties service 5 from Yarmouth
**Pushchairs:** with difficulty.

and Breydon Water itself, not a "broad" as such, is reduced to sand flats at low tide!

This view of Burgh Castle takes in the whole of the walk (courtesy Mike Page).

1 From the church set off south along the track beside the churchyard, following signs to the castle. You will soon fork right to follow a grassy path across a field, then go through a kissing gate and continue your direction, still roughly south. By now the flint ruins of the castle should

*Distant View of the Castle.*

be visible, and you should head straight for it. Please spend some time enjoying the castle, and reading the information boards. This is a splendid spot for a picnic. Burgh Castle was built in the late third or early fourth centuries as part of a string of forts around the south and east coasts. Three of the four sides of the fort are probably at their original height, an achievement matched by few other Roman sites in Britain. The flint and mortar walls of the fort are in the care

*Burgh Castle Church.*

of English Heritage, but the Norfolk Archaeological Trust owns the fort, most of the surrounding farmland and an adjacent area of reed beds. The property in all covers 90 acres (37 hectares). There can be few ancient monuments in East Anglia with a more striking location.

*Church Farm.*

*Castle walls.*

(2) When you wish to leave, head for the opposite corner of the fort to where you entered ie the south-west corner, down a shallow flight of steps, then turn right to head north along the Angles Way, past the reeds. These reed beds provide a breeding ground for bearded tits, reed and sedge warblers and water rail, and many yellow wagtails roost here in late summer and early autumn. Marsh and Hen Harriers are found here in winter and

there have been sightings of bittern and Cetti's warbler.

(3) At the end of the path, turn right at the signpost, and then you can, if you wish, follow the path back to your car. You will have walked about 1 mile.

However, for an attractive addition to your jorney, before walking up the path to the car park, turn left to continue along the Angles Way as it

heads north-west across the marshes. You will soon be able to see the river, and this is the point where the River Yare, which goes broadly west to Norwich (and beyond), splits off from the River Waveney, which goes south-west then broadly west to soon form the boundary between Norfolk and Suffolk. These two rivers flow into the southern tip of Breydon Water, where-as the River Bure flows into the north-ern tip, so the last couple of miles from Breydon Water to the North Sea

*You can see the Berney Arms pub – so isolated that it can only be reached by river, the occasional train (the track is just across the river from your path), or by foot across the marshes (at least 2 miles from Halvergate).*

is really a combination of all 3 rivers! You will soon be on the riverbank path beside the Yare as it starts to bend right to head east into Great Yarmouth. The views here across Halvergate Marshes are fabulous.

(4) After a while you will need to turn round and re-trace your steps back to the car park, as this part of the walk is not circular.

*Reeds – fine thatching material.*

Berney Arms pub.

View north Across Breydon Water.